W9-CPZ-942

ŽIDOVSKÉ
MUZEUM
PRAHA

I HAVE NOT SEEN A BUTTERFLY
AROUND HERE

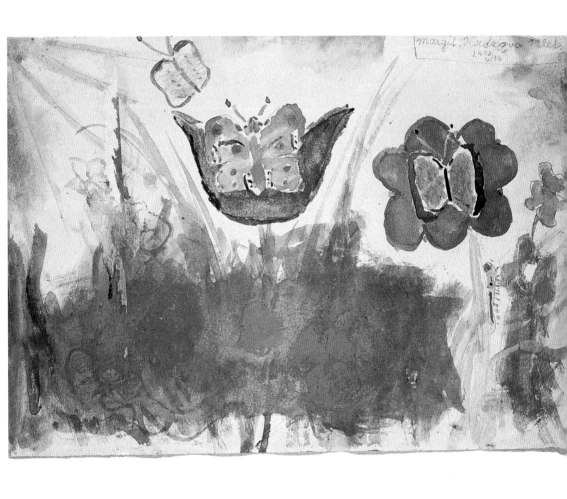

MARGIT KORETZOVÁ, 8.4.1933 – 4.10.1944

I have not seen a butterfly around here

CHILDREN'S DRAWINGS AND POEMS FROM TEREZÍN

THE BUTTERFLY

The last, the very last,
So richly, brightly, dazzlingly yellow.
Perhaps if the sun's tears would sing .
against a white stone…

Such, such a yellow
Is carried lightly 'way up high.
It went away I'm sure because it wished
to kiss the world goodbye.

For seven weeks I've lived in here,
Penned up inside this ghetto
But I have found my people here.
The dandelions call to me
And the white chestnut candles in the court.
Only I never saw another butterfly.

That butterfly was the last one.
Butterflies don't live in here,
In the ghetto.

PAVEL FRIEDMANN, 7. 1. 1921 – 29. 9. 1944

ROBERT BONDY, 1.5.1932 – 6.10.1944

In Bohemia, there is a strange place called Terezín, some 60 kilometers from Prague. It was founded by order of Emperor Joseph II of Austria, 200 years ago and named after his mother, Maria Theresa. This walled-in fortress was constructed on plans drafted by Italian military engineers and has 12 ramparts which enclose the town in the shape of a star. It was to have been a fortress and it became a sleepy army garrison dominated by the barracks, where the homes of the inhabitants were simply put up with. There were homes, taverns, a post office, a bank and a brewery. There was a church as well, built in a sober style and belonging to the barracks as part of the army community. The little town seemed to have been forced onto the countryside, a lovely countryside without either high mountains or dizzy cliffs, without deep ravines or swift rivers... only blue hills, green meadows, fruit trees and tall poplars.

Today, a shadow still lingers above this little town as though funeral wagons still drive along its streets, as though the dust still eddies in the town square, stirred by a thousand footsteps. Today, it seems sometimes as though from every corner, from every stairway and from every corridor, peer human faces, gaunt, exhausted, with eyes full of fear.

During the war years, Terezín was a place of famine and of fear. Somewhere far away, in Berlin, men in uniforms had held meetings. These men decided to exterminate all the Jews in Europe, and because they were used to doing things thoroughly with the calculated, cool passion of a murderer, they worked out plans in which they fixed the country, the place and the timetable as well as the stopping places on that road to death. One of these stopping places was Terezín.

It was meant to be a model camp which foreigners could be shown, and it was termed a ghetto. At first, Jews from Bohemia and Moravia were brought to Terezín, but finally they came from all over Europe and from hence were shipped further east to the gas chambers and ovens. Everything in this small town was false, invented: every one of its inhabitants was condemned in advance to die. It was only a tunnel without an outlet. Those who contrived this trap and put it on their map, with its fixed timetable of life and death, knew all about it. They knew its future as well. Those who were brought here in crowded railroad coaches and stockcars after days and days of cruelty, of humiliation, of offense, of beatings and of theft, knew very little about it. Some of them believed the murderers' falsehoods, that they could sit out the war here in quiet safety. Others came to Terezín already crushed, yet with a spark of hope that even so, perhaps they might escape their destiny. There were also those who knew that Terezín was only one station in a short timetable and that is why they tried so hard to keep at least themselves alive and perhaps their family. And those who were good and honorable, endeavored to keep the children alive, the aged and the ailing. All were finally deceived and the same fate awaited all of them.

But the children who were brought here knew nothing. They came from places where they had already known humiliation; they had been expelled from the schools. They had sewn stars on their hearts, on their jackets and blouses, and were only allowed to play in the cemeteries. That wasn't so bad, if you look at it with the eyes of a child, even when they heard their parents' lamentations, even when they heard strange words charged with horror such as mapping, registration and transport. When they were herded with their parents into the ghetto, when they had to sleep on the concrete floors in crowded garrets or clamber up three-tiered bunks, they began to look around and quickly understood the strange world in which they had to live. They saw reality, but they still maintained their childish outlook, an outlook of truth which distinguishes between night and day and cannot be confused with false hopes and the shadowplay of an imaginary life.

And so they lived, locked within walls and courtyards. This was their world, a world of color and shadow, of hunger and of hope.

The children played in the barracks yard and the courtyards of the one-time homes. Sometimes they were permitted to breathe a little fresh air upon the ramparts. From the age of 14, they had to work, to live the life of an adult. Sometimes they went beyond the walls to work in the gardens and they were no more considered to be children. The smaller ones acted out their fairy tales and even children's operas. But they did not know that they too, as well as the grown-ups, had been used deceitfully, in an effort to convince a commission of foreigners from the Red Cross that Terezín was a place where adults and children alike could live. Secretly, they studied and they drew pictures. Three months, half a year, one or two years, depending on one's luck, because transports came and went continually, headed east into nothingness.

From these 15,000 children which for a time played and drew pictures and studied, only 100 came back. They saw everything, that grown-ups saw. They saw the endless queues in front of the canteens, they saw the funeral carts used to carry bread and the human beings harnessed to pull them. They saw the SS-men strolling on pavements and the men who had to raise their caps to them and the women who had to bow low to them. They saw the infirmaries which seemed like a paradise to them and funerals which were only a gathering-up of coffins. They listened to a speech made up of a hodgepodge of expressions like „bonke", „shlajska", „shahojista", and they learned to speak this language. They heard the shouts of the SS-men at roll call and the meek mumblings of prayers in the barracks where the grown-ups lived.

But the chidren saw too what the grown-ups didn't want to see, the beauties beyond the village gates, the green meadows and the bluish hills, the ribbon of highway reaching off into the distance and the imagined road marker pointing toward

„Praha", the animals, the birds, the butterflies – all this was beyond the village walls and they could look at it only from afar, from the barracks windows and from the ramparts of the fort. They saw things too that grown-ups could not see – princesses with coronets, evil wizards and witches, jesters and bugs with human faces, a land of happiness where, for an admission of 1 Kč, there was everything to be had – cookies, candy, a roast pig stuck with a fork, where milk and sodapop trickled. They saw too the rooms they'd lived in at home, with curtains at the window and a kitten and a saucer of milk. But they transported it to Terezín. There had to be a fence and a lot of pots and pans, because there was supposed to be food in every pot and pan.

All this they drew and painted and many other things besides; they loved to paint and draw, from morning till evening.

But when they wrote poems, it was something else again. Here one finds words about „painful Terezín", about „the little girl who got lost". These told of longings to go away somewhere where there are kinder people: there are old grandfathers gnawing stale bread and rotten potatoes for lunch, here was a „longing for home" and fear. Yes, fear came to them and they could tell of it in their poems, knowing that they were condemned. Perhaps they knew it better than the adults.

There were 15,000 of them and 100 came back. You are looking at their drawings now after many years, when that world of hunger, fear and horror seems to us almost like a cruel fairy tale about evil wizards, witches and cannibals. The drawings and poems – that is all that is left of these children, for their ashes have long since sifted across the fields around Auschwitz. Their signatures are here and some of the drawings are inscribed with the year, their group and time. Of those who signed their names, it has been possible to find out a few facts: the year and place of their birth, the number of their transport to Terezín and to Auschwitz and then the year of their death. For most of them, it was 1944, the next to last year of World War II.

But their drawings and their poems speak to us; these are their voices which have been preserved, voices of reminder, of truth and of hope.

We are publishing them not as dry documents out of thousands such witnesses in a sea of suffering, but in order to honor the memory of those who created these colors and these words. That's the way these children probably would have wanted it when they overtook death.

JIŘÍ WEIL

EVA WOLLSTEINEROVÁ, 24.1.1931 – 23.10.1944

AT TEREZÍN

When a new child comes
Everything seems strange to him.
What, on the ground I have to lie?
Eat black potatoes? No! Not I!
I've got to stay? It's dirty here!
The floor-why, look, it's dirt, I fear!
And I'm supposed to sleep on it?
I'll get all dirty!

Here the sound of shouting, cries,
And oh, so many flies.
Everyone knows flies carry disease.
Oooh, something bit me! Wasn't that a bedbug?
Here in Terezín, life is hell.
And when I'll go home again, I can't yet tell.

"TEDDY"

IT ALL DEPENDS ON HOW YOU LOOK AT IT

I.

Terezín is full of beauty.
It's in your eyes now clear
And through the street the tramp
Of many marching feet I hear.

In the ghetto at Terezín,
It looks that way to me,
Is a square kilometer of earth
Cut off from the world that's free.

II.

Death, after all, claims everyone,
You find it everywhere.
It catches up with even those
Who wear their noses in the air.

The whole, wide world is ruled
With a certain justice, so
That helps perhaps to sweeten
The poor man's pain and woe.

MIROSLAV KOŠEK, 30.3.1932 – 19.10.1944

14

SONJA FISCHEROVÁ, 16.3.1931 – SURVIVED

MAN PROPOSES,
GOD DISPOSES

I.

Who was helpless back in Prague,
And who was rich before,
He's a poor soul here in Terezín,
His body's bruised and sore.

II.

Who was toughened up before,
He'll survive these days.
But who was used to servants
Will sink into his grave.

KOLÉBA : MIROSLAV KOŠEK   30.3.1932 – 19.10.1944
          HANUŠ LÖWY   29.6.1931 – 4.10.1944
          BACHNER

ANNA KLAUSNEROVÁ, 23.7.1932 – 12.10.1944

EVA MEITNEROVÁ, 1.5.1931 – 28.10.1944

MARIKA FRIEDMANNOVÁ, 6.8.1932 – 4.10.1944

VILÉM EISNER, 4.6.1931 – 4.10.1944

PAIN STRIKES SPARKS ON ME,
THE PAIN OF TEREZIN

Fifteen beds. Fifteen charts with names,
Fifteen people without a family tree.
Fifteen bodies for whom torture is medicine and pills,
Beds over which the crimson blood of ages spills.
Fifteen bodies which want to live here.
Thirty eyes, seeking quietness.
Bald heads which gape from out the prison.
The holiness of the suffering, which is none
                                of my business.

The loveliness of air, which day after day
Smells of strangeness and carbolic,
The nurses which carry thermometers
Mothers who grope after a smile.
Food is such a luxury here.
A long, long night, and a brief day.

But anyway, I don't want to leave
The lighted rooms and the burning cheeks,
Nurses who leave behind them only a shadow
To help the little sufferers.

I'd like to stay here, a small patient,
Waiting the doctor's daily round,
Until after a long, long time, I'd be well again.

Then I'd like to live
And go back home again.

UNKNOWN AUTHOR

TEREZÍN

That bit of filth in dirty walls,
And all around barbed wire,
And 30,000 souls who sleep
Who once will wake
And once will see
Their own blood spilled.

I was once a little child,
Three years ago.
That child who longed for other worlds.
But now I am no more a child
For I have learned to hate.
I am a grown-up person now,
I have known fear,

Bloody words and a dead day then,
That's something different than bogie man!

But anyway, I still believe I only sleep today,
That I'll wake up, child again, and start to laugh and play.
I'll go back to childhood sweet like a briar rose,
Like a bell which wakes us from a dream,
Like a mother with an ailing child
Loves him with aching woman's love.
How tragic, then, is youth which lives
With enemies, with gallows ropes,
How tragic, then, for children on your lap
To say: this for the good, that for the bad.

Somewhere, far away out there, childhood
                              sweetly sleeps,
Along that path among the trees,
There o'er that house
Which was once my pride and joy.
There my mother gave me birth into this world
So I could weep…

In the flame of candles by my bed, I sleep
And once perhaps I'll understand
That I was such a little thing,
As little as this song.

These 30,000 souls who sleep
Among the trees will wake,
Open eyes
And because they see
A lot

They'll fall asleep again…

HANUŠ HACHENBURG, 12.7.1929 – 10.-12.7.1944

YES, THAT'S THE WAY THINGS ARE

I.

In Terezín in the so-called park
A queer old granddad sits
Somewhere there in the so-called park.
He wears a beard down to his lap
And on his head, a little cap.

II.

Hard crusts he crumbles in his gums,
He's only got one single tooth.
My poor old man with working gums,
Instead of soft rolls, lentil soup.
My poor old grey-beard!

KOLÉBA: MIROSLAV KOŠEK 30.3.1932 – 19.10.1944
HANUŠ LÖWY   29.6.1931 – 4.10.1944
BACHNER

MARGIT ULLRICHOVÁ, 18.6.1931 – 16.10.1944

RUTH GUTMANNOVÁ, 13.4.1930 – 6.10.1944

MARIANNA ROSENZWEIGOVÁ, 7.11.1929 – SURVIVED

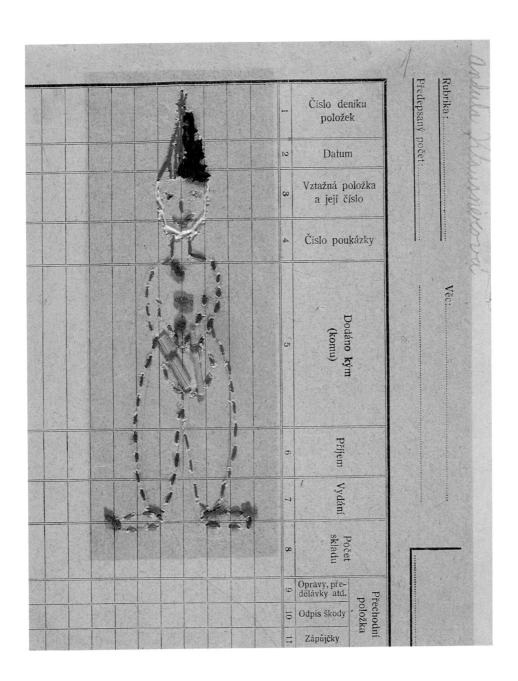

	1	Číslo deníku položek
2	Datum
3	Vztažná položka a její číslo
4	Číslo poukázky
5	Dodáno kým (komu)
6	Příjem
7	Vydání
8	Počet skladu
9	Opravy, pře- dělávky atd.
10	Odpis škody
11	Zápůjčky
	Přechodní položka

ANNA KLAUSNEROVÁ, 23.7.1932 – 12.10.1944

THE LITTLE MOUSE

I.

A mousie sat upon a shelf,
Catching fleas in his coat of fur.
But he couldn't catch her – What chagrin! –
She'd hidden 'way inside his skin.
He turned and wriggled, knew no rest,
That flea was such a nasty pest!

II.

His daddy came
And searched his coat.
He caught the flea and off he ran
To cook her in the frying pan.
The little mouse cried, „Come and see!
For lunch we've got a nice, fat flea!"

KOLÉBA: MIROSLAV KOŠEK 30.3.1932 – 19.10.1944
         HANUŠ LÖWY   29.6.1931 – 4.10.1944
         BACHNER

HOMESICK

I've lived in the ghetto here more than a year,
In Terezín, in the black town now,
And when I remember my old home so dear,
I can love it more than I did, somehow.

Ah, home, home,
Why did they tear me away?
Here the weak die easy as a feather
And when they die, they die forever.

I'd like to go back home again,
I makes me think of sweet spring flowers.
Before, when I used to live at home,
It never seemed so dear and fair.

I remember now those golden days...
But maybe I'll be going there soon again.

People walk along the street,
You see at once on each you meet
That there's a ghetto here,
A place of evil and of fear.

There's little to eat and much to want,
Where bit by bit, it's horror to live.
But no one must give up!
The world turns and times change.

Yet we all hope the time will come
When we'll go home again.
Now I know how dear it is
And often I remember it.

UNKNOWN AUTHOR

HELGA POLLAKOVÁ, 28.5.1930 – SURVIVED

UNKNOWN AUTHOR

ROBERT BONDY, 1.5.1932 – 6.10.1944

IRENA KARPELESOVÁ, 30.12.1930 – 23.10.1944

NIGHT IN THE GHETTO

Another day has gone for keeps
Into the bottomless pit of time.
Again it has wounded a man, held captive
by his brethren.
He longs for bandages of dusk,
For soft hands to shield the eyes
From all the horrors that stare by day.
But in the ghetto, darkness too is kind
To weary eyes which all day long
Have had to watch.

Dawn crawls again along the ghetto streets
Embracing all who walk this way.
Only a car like a greeting from a long-gone world
Boggles up the dark with fiery eyes –
That sweet darkness that falls upon the soul
And heals those wounds illumined by the day. . .
Along the streets come light ranks of people
Like a long black ribbon, loomed with gold.

UNKNOWN AUTHOR

QUESTIONS, AND AN ANSWER

What use are human art and science?
Beauty of women, fresh as May?
What use, a world that's mere illusion?
What use, the sun, when there's no day?

What is God for? Only to chasten?
Or a new humankind to fashion?
Or are we merely beasts who suffer
To rot beneath the yoke of passion?

What is life for, if life is torment,
The world a rampart against light?
Know, son, all things are as they are here
That you may be a man! And fight!

HANUŠ HACHENBURG, 12.7.1929 – 10.-12.7.1944

FEAR

Today the ghetto knows a different fear,
Close in its grip, Death wields an icy scythe.
An evil sickness spreads a terror in its wake,
The victims of its shadow weep and writhe.

Today a father's heartbeat tells his fright
And mothers bend their heads into their hands.
Now children choke and die with typhus here,
A bitter tax is taken from their bands.

My heart still beats inside my breast
While friends depart for other worlds.
Perhaps it's better – who can say?
Than watching this, to die today?

No, no, my God, we want to live!
Not watch our numbers melt away.
We want to have a better world,
We want to work – we must not die!

EVA PICKOVÁ, 15.5.1929 – 18.12.1943

RUTH GUTMANNOVÁ, 13.4.1930 – 6.10.1944

38

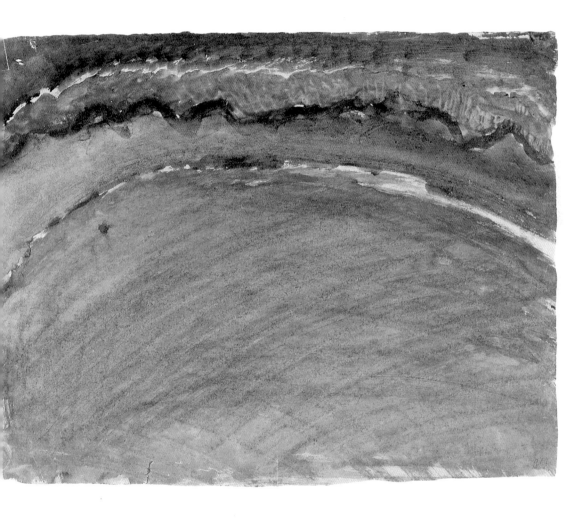

UNKNOWN AUTHOR

RUTH HEINOVÁ, 19.2.1934 – 23.10.1944

UNKNOWN AUTHOR

41

SOŇA WALDSTEINOVÁ, 28.11.1926 – SURVIVED

TO OLGA

Listen!
The boat whistle has sounded now
And we must sail
Out toward an unknown port.
Listen!
Now it's time.

We'll sail a long, long way
And dreams will turn to truth.
Oh, how sweet the name Morocco!
Listen!
Now it's time.

The wind sings songs of far away,
Just look up to heaven
And think about the violets.
Listen!
Now it's time.

ALENA SYNKOVÁ, 24.9.1926 – SURVIVED

DORIS ZDEKAUEROVÁ, 15.12.1932 – 16.10.1944

FORGOTTEN

You wanton, quiet memory that haunts me all the while
In order to remind me of her whom love I send.
Perhaps when you caress me sweetly, I will smile,
You are my confidante today, my very dearest friend.

You sweet remembrance, tell a fairy tale
About my girl who's lost and gone, you see.
Tell, tell the one about the golden grail
And call the swallow, bring her back to me.

Fly somewhere back to her and ask her, soft and low,
If she thinks of me sometimes with love,
If she is well and ask her too before you go
If I am still her dearest, precious dove.

And hurry back, don't lose your way,
So I can think of other things,
But you were too lovely, perhaps, to stay.
I loved you once. Goodbye, my love!

ZDENĚK OHRENSTEIN, 10.1.1929 – SURVIVED

EVA PREISSOVÁ, 15.1.1932 – SURVIVED

THE GARDEN

A little garden,
Fragrant and full of roses.
The path is narrow
And a little boy walks along it.

A little boy, a sweet boy,
Like that growing blossom.
When the blossom comes to bloom,
The little boy will be no more.

FRANTA BASS, 4.9.1930 – 28.10.1944

MARIANNA LANGOVÁ, 27.2.1932 – 6.10.1944

JOSEF NOVÁK, 25.10.1931 – 18.5.1944

EVA RIESSOVÁ, 25.7.1931 – SURVIVED

RUTH GUTMANNOVÁ, 13.4.1930 – 6.10.1944

NELLY SILVÍNOVÁ, 21.12.1931 – 4.10.1944

RŮŽENA ZENTNEROVÁ, 26.3.1933 – 4.10.1944

ILLNESS

A sad silence in the room.
In the centre a bed and a table.
In the bed lies a boy burning with fever.
Beside him his mother sits reading
                          from a book.
She reads him a beautiful fairy-tale
And at once his fever is cooled.

THE WORLD

A great globe turns about
Around the sun, around the stars.
The globe has a name,
The globe is called The World.

People live on this globe,
Beasts live their wild lives there.
The globe has been turning for ages,
The globe is surely dying.

BAGPIPES

A little table stands bear to the door,
An old man sits on a stool with his bagpipes,
Tapping out with his foot the rhythm of the pipes.
In six years' time he may no longer be living.

I AM A JEW

I am a Jew, a Jew I shall remain.
Even if I die of hunger
I will not give up my nation,
I will fight always
For my nation, on my honour.
I will never be ashamed
Of my nation, on my honour.

I am proud of my nation,
A nation most worthy of honour.
I shall always be oppressed,
I shall always live again.

THE ROSE

The rose, the rose, how marvellously
sweet it smells.
The scent wafts far
over the countryside,
This rose, this rose.

The sweet, familiar scent
Drifts over the sorrowful fields,
Alas, already it withers,
The rose, the rose.

The rose is already faded,
The scent dies,
That wonderful fragrance,
That resplendent rose.

HOME

I gaze and gaze into the wide world,
Into the wide and distant world,
I gaze and gaze towards the south-east,
I gaze and gaze towards my home.

I gaze towards home,
Towards the town where I was born,
My town, my native town,
How gladly I would return to you.

THE OLD HOUSE

The old house stands here forsaken,
In silence, in slumber.
How beautiful this house was once,
How beautiful then, standing here.

It is forsaken,
Mouldering in silence.
Alas for the house!
Alas for the times!

FRANTA BASS, 4.9.1930 – 28.10.1944

UNKNOWN AUTHOR

MARIE FANTLOVÁ, 16.10.1930 – 23.10.1944

EVA HELLEROVÁ, 19.1.1931 – 15.12.1943

RUTH GUTMANNOVÁ, 13.4.1930 – 6.10.1944

GUSTAV ZWEIG, 31.7.1930 – 4.10.1944

60

REFLECTIONS

I stood at the corner, and stared in at the window,
There where heart is severed from heart.
The Hades' shades, meagre and wretched, lay on the beds
And one of those poor idiots lifted a hand, calling:
„Mother!
Mother – come, and let's play together!
We'll kiss, and talk, we two together!"

Poor souls, madmen, figurines,
So are they all, these who go half-naked,
Shivering with cold, as though they must cry out
Before the days surge in and overwhelm them.

„Mother, cherish your child, I am a leaf ripe for falling,
See how I cower here shivering, I am so cold!"
Like a dreadful chorale it echoed through the barracks,
And I – torn asunder by the whirlwind, was singing with it.

HANUŠ HACHENBURG, 12.7.1929 – 10.-12.7.1944

MILAN BIENENFELD, 28.3.1930 – 18.5.1944

UNKNOWN AUTHOR

RUTH SCHÄCHTEROVÁ, 24.8.1930 – 18.5.1944

I'd like to go away alone
Where there are other, nicer people,
Somewhere into the far unknown,
There, where no one kills another.

Maybe more of us,
A thousand strong,
Will reach this goal
Before too long.

ALENA SYNKOVÁ, 24.9.1926 – SURVIVED

LEA POLLAKOVÁ, 21.3.1930 – 18.5.1944

HANUŠ WEINBERG, 18.8.1931 – 15.12.1943

BIRDSONG

He doesn't know the world at all
Who stays in his nest and doesn't go out.
He doesn't know what birds know best
Nor what I want to sing about,
That the world is full of loveliness.

When dewdrops sparkle in the grass
And earth's aflood with morning light,
A blackbird sings upon a bush
To greet the dawning after night.
Then I know how fine it is to live.

Hey, try to open up your heart
To beauty; go to the woods someday
And weave a wreath of memory there.
Then if the tears obscure your way
You'll know how wonderful it is
To be alive.

UNKNOWN AUTHOR

JOSEF NOVÁK, 25.10.1931 – 18.5.1944

DORIS WEISEROVÁ, 17.5.1932 – 4.10.1944

WHILE ...

Make no impatient move, my son, my young green tree,
While yet your eyes have hardly seen the day,
And in your pram these reins still hold you carefully.
Grow big and wise before you fly away.

You mustn't be in haste, your world is still new-born,
You can't have everything the days reveal.
The world's a thorny place, you may get pricked and torn,
You need a hero's heart, a shield of steel.

When you are grown a man, to build the world anew,
Your soul will sink, worn down by doubts and fears,
And sick and fainting, turn with longing to renew
That briefest fairy-tale, the childhood years.

Make no impatient move, my son, my young green tree.
Wait, wait for all, content to live in measure.
Leave all these foolish longings, they're just vanity.
You need not want, while you are mother's treasure.

ZDENĚK OHRENSTEIN, 10.1.1929 – SURVIVED

JIŘÍ RIES, 4.9.1933 – 4.10.1944

SOME DAY

Some day we shall outrun this hour,
Some day there will be comfort for us,
And hope again burst into flower,
And peace and guardian care restore us.
The jug of tears will break and spill,
And death be ordered: 'Hush, be still!'

The true dawn will come at last,
Wine from water be revealed,
Some day all our tears be past,
Some day all our wounds be healed.
All our slavish chains, some day,
God will smite and strike away.

Some day Herod, mad with fear
Shall go raving to his ending,
And the Shepherd-king appear,
In royal purple robes ascending,
He who once suffered, even as we,
By King Saul's hate and cruelty.

Some day all sorrows will take flight,
This life thus wretched and laborious.
The saviour will appear in might,
With his all-conquering power victorious.
Some day, if God will, we'll stand
Free men in the promised land.

Some day the aloes will bloom fair,
Some day the palms bear fruit again,
Some day the burden of despair
Be lifted to assuage our pain.
And in God's house we'll live anew.
Some day all these things will be true!

IVO KATZ, 11.4.1932 – 18.12.1943

73

GABI FREIOVÁ, 1.1.1933 – 18.5.1944

ANITA SPITZOVÁ, 6.1.1933 – 4.10.1944

HANUŠ FISCHL, 26.9.1933 – 6.10.1944

The poor thing stands there vainly.
Vainly he strains his voice.
Perhaps he'll die. Then can you say
How beautiful is the world today?

ZDENĚK OHRENSTEIN, 10.1.1929 – SURVIVED

CHILDREN'S DRAWINGS AND POEMS FROM THE TEREZÍN GHETTO

The drawings and poems drawn and written by children in the Terezín ghetto, established by the Nazis as their temporary dwelling-place before their journey to death, have addressed and moved us for nearly half a century now. They became memorials of thousands of children who were not permitted to reach adult age and who have not their own little grave with a real memorial anywhere.

The drawings number over 4,000 and there are hundreds of poems and other literary forms. Still today very few people know them and even in this publication we can acquaint you with only a negligible fraction of them. After the elapse of many years the Jewish Museum in Prague is returning to this theme which, in our opinion, remains vital. Our wish is to make it known also to the newly born generation, which is fortunate in that the period during which these drawings were drawn and the poems written is ancient history for them. They were drawn and written by children in order to express their joy and their sorrow and to share their memories, longings, fears and hopes. They believed in a happy tomorrow and had no idea that the death sentence had already been written and signed in respect of most of them.

In the years 1941 to 1945 the Terezín ghetto in the former fortress garrison town in North Bohemia was their involuntary and temporary home. Some of them were here for a short time only and did not have time to pick up a pencil and draw a picture or write a poem. The luckier ones, if one can call life in a concentration camp luck, stayed at Terezín longer and left us their artistic and literary heritage. Most of them were gradually deported from the ghetto to extermination camps and ghettos in the „east", the last of them at the end of October 1944. Only very few children lived to see the liberation of Terezín.

The longing of children and youth for active occupation of their minds, expressed among other things by artistic and literary work, was actually quite natural in the wholly special environment of the Terezín ghetto.

The Terezín ghetto was one of the many elements of the gearing on the way to realization of the monstrous Nazi plan – the so-called final solution of the Jewish question – which ended in the murdering of six million European Jews. The position of Terezín was, however, specific and the ghetto itself differed from the ghettos on eastern territories and, naturally, also from the extermination camps, which were the scene of the final phase of the final solution, i.e. to the murder of the victims. Although living conditions in the Terezín ghetto were more bearable than in the previously mentioned camps and ghettos the death rate here was relatively high. About 25% of the Terezín prisoners died in the ghetto – of hunger, exhaustion and spreading infections. Similarly as all other concentration camps Terezín thus also fulfilled a decimation function to a considerable extent. The Terezín ghetto had, furthermore, the character of a transit camp, a place of a temporary sojourn. The prevailing majority of the prisoners lived here only for a time. After a shorter or longer period they were deported to extermination camps and ghettos in eastern occupied territories. For most of them this journey meant certain death. Third, the Terezín ghetto played a wholly specific role in the propagandist plans of the Nazis. A spa for old people – such was the way it was presented on the occasion of deportations from Germany. Later, when their faith in victory in the war faded, they tried to cleanse themselves in front of their own eyes and those of the public and in the course of negotiations which they hoped would end to their own benefit. In that period Terezín was exploited in a significant way. After long and well-thought-out preparations a comedy was played which was intended to present Terezín as an exemplary Jewish settlement in which Jews lived quite well. This tragic farce took place in the summer of 1944. Both before and after it many thousands were sent from Terezín to Auschwitz.

Human beings lived in this environment. Rid of their freedom, social status, calling, property, family life and all privacy. They were rid of all human rights and were finally to be rid of their life, because they were born as Jews. They were often hungry and many of them had to work hard for long hours. They lived on three-storeyed bunks in the crowded rooms of the barracks and in all the interiors of the homes of civilians, or on the floors of attics or former horse stables. They suffered due to a lack of hygiene and fell victim to diseases for which there were no suitable remedies. A constant stream of transports flowed to the ghetto and at certain times the number of its inhabitants many times exceeded the normal state. At the same time, however, another stream of transports left Terezín. People lived in constant fear of being included in a transport and of their forced departure or that of their near ones for the unknown.

In spite of all this most of them did not succumb to the suffering and oppression to which they were subjected every day and succeeded in taking every opportunity to liberate themselves from their daily mortification. In this abnormal environment they used all their remaining energy to create something unseen, unexpected and fascinating – a many-sided and rich cultural life. In the ghetto, wholly isolated from the rest of the world and torn away from normal life, they performed the most varied theatre genres and organized concerts of serious and mood music. Lectures were given and amateurs sketched and painted, musical works were composed and poems and prose were written.

At first theatre performances, concerts and recitation or social evenings were realized in secret, later being more or less suffered and, finally, even fostered and exploited in the framework of the propagation aims of the Nazis. Apart from the final phase, all these events took place in attics and yards, with a lack of quality musical instruments and with stage sets and costumes made of rags and papers, but with the enormous enthusiasm of the actors and spectators, in the evening after a whole day of exhausting work.

It is not surprising that this environment of want, suffering and fear on one hand and enthusiasm, strength of will and cultural activity on the other hand also influenced the life and creative endeavours of the child prisoners of the ghetto.

Thus even children drew pictures, wrote poems and published their magazines. They kept diaries and recorded things in notebooks. Even children gave or watched theatre performances. And at the same time even they, similarly as the adults, often suffered from hunger, crowded living conditions and disease – and died. In most cases they lived apart from their parents. They missed them, but on the other hand life in the collective of a home for children or youth was a gift in the given environment, successfully prepared for them by the adult prisoners in the ghetto. They were spared from a view of a great deal of human suffering and the tragedies which took place in the barracks of the adults. Beautiful friendships originated in the homes and the children learned tolerance and unselfishness in their collective. They, too, lived in fear of the transports to the east. The departure of their friends caused them even greater suffering, however. Their poems often manifest a longing to follow after them and to meet them again somewhere in the unknown. Even in the environment of the ghetto, in the collective of a home, their childish soul succeeded in creating its own children's world – a world which contained many interesting things and friends and a great deal of fun. And, in addition, active work which allowed them at least for a moment to forget their everyday life in the camp – illegal teaching, drawing lessons, lectures and theatre.

The originators of the drawings are more often girls of 10 to 15 years of age. We do not know if girls had a greater need to express their feelings through artistic activity. We are rather inclined to suppose that drawing lessons were realized in greater numbers and more regularly in the L 410 home for girls. After all, their organizer, the teacher of drawing to the children of Terezín, the outstanding artist Friedl Dicker-Brandejs, also lived there. In spite of this, however, boys also drew pictures under her guidance.

During their drawing lessons the children were divided into groups. F.D.-Brandejs gave them individual themes to express artistically and mostly left them to work independently in order to give free rein to their fantasy. Thus certain thematic cycles originated in whose framework whole groups of drawings have been preserved. The various cut out pictures, pictures created by sticking cuttings on paper and pictures embroidered on paper as well as the different free compositions are very interesting from the artistic aspect. Especially valuable for us today are the drawings which clearly show the gentle guidance and sometimes experienced touch of the artist and teacher. We can see a whole number of drawings in which the children learned to use various techniques, perspective and the grading of colour shades. In this way many immensely interesting colour compositions originated, often resembling original abstract art. In this case the influence of the teacher is very pronounced. In this case the children really learned to create drawings under her experienced hand. In another large series the children expressed a concrete theme with given contents and once again several drawings with the same theme have been preserved in each case. In this case the children worked somewhat more freely, clearly without the intervention of F. D.-Brandejs. As contemporaries testify, the teacher did not set any special theme during the so-called free lessons. Every child drew what momentarily occurred to it. The purpose of these lessons was to foster the ability of selfexpression in the pupils and thus give rein to their mental faculties.

From the aspect of contents the drawings are divided into two parts. In the first of them we find, apart from the mentioned drawing exercises, compositions, etc., subjects which most children draw also in their normal life. The children of Terezín also drew landscapes, city streets, their family, flowers and animals, children's games and fairy-tale scenes. They naturally did not exhaust these subjects from their every-day experiences, but only from their memories. The second, much smaller group of drawings contains portrayals of the children's experiences at the camp. Dormitories, bunks, the Terezín barracks, transport and many sadder scenes. The fact that the joyful drawings are much greater in number witnesses the strength of the spirit of a child and the influence of the Terezín children's teacher.

F. D.-Brandejs preferred to work with a larger group of children, who helped one another, mutually judged all the drawings and learned how to show regard for others. She chose a different approach when she worked with younger children, leaving them to draw entirely on their own on the basis of the principle that a young child should not be disturbed at play and when seeking its own way and also that there is no point in teaching it. She considered the drawing and painting of small children to be one of their main media of expression. In her opinion, however, an older child begins to be dissatisfied with its expressional media at a certain age. Its world of fantasy fades into the background and it begins to show interest in the real world. At this point a form of teaching comes to the fore, but it must not obstruct the freedom of a child when it is working.

The children had very few drawing aids at their disposal. They lent what they had to one another and took it in turn to work. They drew everything that was momentarily at hand. Apart from rare quarto it was expecially ordinary paper of various qualities and sizes, sometimes even packing and blotting paper and forms. The children used pencils, crayons, coloured pencils and water colours. Very often it was necessary to use a pencil even when it was not suitable for the given material or theme. Apart from very successful drawings many non-artistic ones have been preserved. They are the drawings of children who, it is true, had no special artistic talent, but nevertheless thoroughly enjoyed drawing.

For F. D.-Brandejs the drawing lessons were not merely a mechanical way of keeping the children busy and it was not her aim to educate future artists through them. She tried not to direct the children's ideas, because she did not want to lose the possibility of penetrating into their inner world. And so she also used the lessons for the spiritual rehabilitation of the small prisoners. By analyzing their drawings she tried to penetrate into their thoughts and feelings and in the course of further artistic work to secure rest and recreation for them in order to lessen their possible states of stress. Thus for the children drawing was a form of escape from joyless reality. It was a delight and a therapy. F.D.-Brandejs was not only an outstanding artist, but also an exceptional pedagogue, a good psychologist and, above all, a very special person who was loved by all her child pupils.

Contrary to the children's drawings, the greater part of the literature of the Terezín children was written by boys. These works originated in a more elemental manner and have been preserved in large numbers especially in the children's magazines, published in most cases just by boys. In these they also expressed themselves artistically and often accompanied their written works with drawings. The poems, which originated separately, outside the framework of the magazines, were also written more frequently by boys than by girls. This applies whether they were small poems written by the smallest children, often resembling rather naive, charming and often humourous children's nursery rhymes, or real attempts to write poetry made, often successfully, by older boys. However, this branch of activity was not the exclusive domain of boys. Successful poems written by girls have been preserved even if in a small number. These are characterized, however, by a more serious tone. Contrary to the boys, the girls were more inclined to keep autograph albums and personal diaries, often accompanied by drawings. Here again, similarly as in the case of the magazines, we come across combinations of artistic and literary work.

The older writers of poetic texts in particular often reacted very sensitively to the reality of the Terezín ghetto. At the same time, however, their poems are permeated with memories of their lost home and happy childhood as well as with bitterness at being torn away from normal life. They manifest a strong longing to return home and quite realistic ideas of life after their liberation.

The poems and literary works of the Terezín children and youth in general are of a high corresponding value. They are a historical source of the conditions in the ghetto and especially of the life of its children. They afford us an insight into the inner feelings of their authors and an understanding of their feelings as prisoners, their perception of life in the ghetto, their suffering and small childish joys, their fears and their faith in a better future. Many of the poems are also of a high literary value. To date children's literary works from Terezín have unjustly remained in the shadow of the drawings of the Terezín children. It is necessary, however, to regard them as equal and mutally supplementing creations. It is just through their merging that we can understand more about the world of the Terezín children than by a one-sided and separate study of them. The drawings are naturally stronger at first sight and move us more quickly and more easily. In this sense they are certainly irreplaceable. The prevailing majority of the children's literary works were written in the Czech language.

In this publication we have tried to acquaint the reader also with some poems which have not yet been published. Apart from a number of well-known drawings, we have also tried to present less known or wholly unknown ones. We hope that we shall be able to continue in these endeavours in the future.

Disputes are still waged about the number of children and young persons that passed through the Terezín ghetto. At present it is estimated that they numbered about 11,000 children and youngsters up to eighteen years of age. They arrived at the Terezín ghetto with their parents, but sometimes alone, from Bohemia, Moravia and Slovakia and from Germany, Austria, Holland, Denmark and Hungary. Most of them were deported elsewhere from Terezín, in particular to Auschwitz, where they died. Only some of them drew pictures and only some of them wrote poems and contributed to the magazines. But they were all children and they all had their hopes, which in most cases were not fulfilled. Their poems, drawings, magazines, diaries and autograph albums are their common heritage. We know their names, their date of birth and the date of their journey to death. There were thousands of them, from infants up to growing girls and boys and they should not be forgotten.

ANITA FRANKOVÁ

EDITOR'S COMMENTS TO THE DRAWINGS

page 4 (Inventory No 125 520)
MARGIT KORETZOVÁ   born on 8. 4. 1933
deported to the Terezín ghetto on 17. 1. 1942,
deported from Terezín to Auschwitz on 4. 10. 1944.
Water colour on a toned paper – size
28,5 x 20,5 cm, signed in the top right corner:
Margit Koretzová, 11 let *(11 years old)*, L 410/16

page 8 (Inventory No 129 983)
ROBERT BONDY   born on 1. 5. 1932
deported to the Terezín ghetto on 30. 9. 1942,
deported from Terezín to Auschwitz on 6. 10. 1944.
Water colour on a white paper – 27,5 x 21 cm, with
a technical drawing on the reverse side, signed at
the bottom right: R.BONDY, L 417 X

page 12 (Inventory No 129 358)
EVA WOLLSTEINEROVÁ   born on 24. 1. 1931
deported to the Terezín ghetto on 8. 4. 1942,
deported from Terezín to Auschwitz on 23. 10. 1944.
Pencil on a toned paper – „Gate to the Magdeburg
barracks" – 30 x 20 cm, signed at the bottom right:
IV. Wollsteiner Eva

page 15 (Inventory No 125 513)
SONJA FISCHEROVÁ   born on 16. 3. 1931
deported to the Terezín ghetto on 3. 8. 1942,
she has survived.
„The view of the sappers'barracks" – water colour
on a white paper – 21 x 31 cm, signed at the top left
corner: Sonja Fischer XIV

page 17 (Inventory No 131 310)
ANNA KLAUSNEROVÁ   born on 23. 7. 1932
deported to the Terezín ghetto on 2. 7. 1942,
deported from Terezín to Auschwitz on 12. 10. 1944.
„The Seder supper", pastel and pencil on a toned
paper – 30,5 x 20 cm, signed at the top right:
Andula Klausnerová

page 18 (Inventory No 125 422)
EVA MEITNEROVÁ   born on 1. 5. 1931
deported to the Terezín ghetto on 4. 7. 1942,
deported from Terezín to Auschwitz on 28. 10. 1944.
„The Seder supper" – pastel on a toned paper –
30,5 x 20,5 cm, signed at the bottom left:
Meitner Eva, and at the bottom right: skup.
(group) IV. Heim 14

page 19 (Inventory No 129 113)
MARIKA FRIEDMANNOVÁ   born on 6. 8. 1932
deported to the Terezín ghetto on 8. 4. 1942,
from Terezín to Auschwitz on 4. 10. 1944.
„The Seder supper", pastel and pencil on a toned
paper – 30 x 20 cm, signed at the bottom right

corner: Marika Friedmannová, at the reverse side
an unfinished drawing of the same motive

page 20 (Inventory No 129 357)
VILÉM EISNER   born on 4. 6. 1931
deported to the Terezín ghetto on 24. 10. 1942,
deported from Terezín to Auschwitz on 4. 10. 1944.
Water colour – 27,5 x 21 cm, signed at the bottom
right: 13.st. V.T.Eisner

page 25 (Inventory No 130 807)
MARGIT ULLRICHOVÁ   born on 18. 6. 1931
deported to the Terezín ghetto on 9. 6. 1943,
deported from Terezín to Auschwitz on 16. 10. 1944.
Water colour on a toned paper – 21,5 x 15,5 cm,
signed at the bottom right corner: ULLRICH
MARGIT

page 26 (Inventory No 129 723)
RUTH GUTMANNOVÁ   born on 13. 4. 1930
deported to the Terezín ghetto on 17. 1. 1942,
deported from Terezín to Auschwitz on 6. 10. 1944.
Collage on a coloured paper – 25,5 x 18,5 cm,
signed on the reverse side at the bottom right
corner: Gutmann Ruth 2 20 L 410 Heim 28 13
Jahre

page 27 (Inventory No 131 929)
MARIANNA ROSENZWEIGOVÁ   born on 7.11. 1929
deported to the Terezín ghetto on 30. 9. 1942,
she has survived.
Collage on a sheet of paper – 22,5 x 30,5 cm,
signed: Rosenzweig

page 28 (Inventory No 129 789)
ANNA KLAUSNEROVÁ   born on 23. 7. 1932
deported to the Terezín ghetto on 2. 7. 1942,
deported from Terezín to Auschwitz on 12. 10. 1944.
Embroidery on a form – 16,5 x 20 cm, signed at the
bottom right: Andula Klausnerová

page 31 (Inventory No 121 767)
HELGA POLLAKOVÁ   born on 28. 5. 1930
deported to the Terezín ghetto on 23. 1. 1943,
deported from Terezín to Auschwitz on 19. 10. 1944,
she has survived.
Water colour – 25 x 17 cm, signed on the reverse
side: Helga Pollaková Heim 28 Gruppe A 3

page 32 (Inventory No 133 012)
UNKNOWN AUTHOR
Water colour on a sheet of paper – 25 x 20 cm

page 33 (Inventory No 129 976)
ROBERT BONDY   born on 1. 5. 1932
deported to the Terezín ghetto on 30. 9. 1942,
deported from Terezín to Auschwitz on 6. 10. 1944.
Water colour on a used sheet of paper –
27,5 x 21 cm, on the reverse side is a ground plan
of a flat, signed at the bottom right corner: Robert
Bondy L 410 X. Bondy

page 34 (Inventory No 129 209)
IRENA KARPELESOVÁ   born on 30.12. 1930
deported to the Terezín ghetto on 22.12. 1942,
deported from Terezín to Auschwitz on 23.10. 1944.
„Table with a Chanukkah lamp", pastel and pencil
drawing on a toned paper – 25 x 17,5 cm, signed at
the top left corner: Karpeles Irené

page 38 (Inventory No 131 315)
RUTH GUTMANNOVÁ   born on 13. 4. 1930
deported to the Terezín ghetto on 17. 1. 1942,
deported from Terezín to Auschwitz on 6. 10. 1944.
Water colour on the reverse side of a coloured
paper – 20,4 x 25 cm, signed at the bottom right
corner: Gutmann Ruth L 410 H 28

page 39 (Inventory No 133 016)
UNKNOWN AUTHOR
Water colour on a toned paper, 25 x 20 cm

page 40 (Inventory No 129 364)
RUTH HEINOVÁ   born on 19. 2. 1934
deported to the Terezín ghetto on 30. 12. 1942,
deported from Terezín to Auschwitz on 23. 10. 1944.
Pastel – 20 x 16,5 cm, signed at the bottom right:
Ruth Hein

page 41 (Inventory No 173 143)
UNKNOWN AUTHOR
Water colour, 22 x 30 cm, signed (?):
17 Plestivenis Babaš 2 st.

page 42 (Inventory No 131 770)
SOŇA WALDSTEINOVÁ   born on 28. 11. 1926
deported to the Terezín ghetto on 6. 3. 1943,
she has survived.
Water colour on a toned paper – 30 x 22 cm,
signed at the top right: Soňa Waldst.

page 44 (Inventory No 129 371)
DORIS ZDEKAUEROVÁ   born on 15. 12. 1932
deported to the Terezín ghetto on 28. 4. 1942,
deported from Terezín to Auschwitz on 16. 10. 1944.
Crayon on a toned paper – 31,5 x 19 cm, signed on
the top margin: Doris Zdekauerová skup. (group) III

page 46 (Inventory No 129 089)
EVA PREISSOVÁ   born on 15. 1. 1932
deported to the Terezín ghetto on 24. 10. 1942,
she has survived.
Water colour on a toned paper – 29 x 20,5 cm,
signed: Eva Preissová

page 48 (Inventory No 129 874)
MARIANNA LANGOVÁ   born on 27. 2. 1932
deported to the Terezín ghetto on 2. 7. 1942,
deported from Terezín to Auschwitz on 6. 10. 1944.
Water colour on a toned paper – 31,5 x 22,5 cm,
signed at the bottom right corner: Lang
Marianne

page 49 (Inventory No 129 919)
JOSEF NOVÁK   born on 25. 10. 1931
deported to the Terezín ghetto on 24. 4. 1942,
deported from Terezín to Auschwitz on 18. 5. 1944.
Water colour on a white sheet of paper –
28,5 x 21,5 cm, with a technical drawing on the reverse side, signed at the bottom right: HEIM X,
NOVAK J. STUNDE 5

page 50 (Inventory No 133 410)
EVA RIESSOVÁ   born on 25. 7. 1931
deported to the Terezín ghetto on 15. 5. 1942,
she has survived.
Collage on a toned paper – 30 x 24 cm, with
a number of curves drawn on the reverse side,
signed at the bottom left: Riess Eva

page 51 (Inventory No 131 806)
RUTH GUTMANNOVÁ   born on 13. 4. 1930
deported to the Terezín ghetto on 17. 1. 1942,
deported from Terezín to Auschwitz on 6. 10. 1944.
Water colour on a white sheet of paper –
30 x 22 cm, signed on the reverse side at the top
right: Gutmann Ruth L 410, Heim 28 13 Jahre

page 52 (Inventory No 130 951)
NELLY SILVÍNOVÁ   born on 21. 12. 1931
deported to the Terezín ghetto on 10. 8. 1942,
deported from Terezín to Auschwitz on 4. 10. 1944.
Collage – 27,5 x 32,5 cm, with a number of curves
drawn in pencil on the reverse side and signed:
Silvín Nelly

page 53 (Inventory No 129 858)
RŮŽENA ZENTNEROVÁ   born on 26. 3. 1933
deported to the Terezín ghetto on 17. 12. 1941,
deported from Terezín to Auschwitz on 4. 10. 1944.
Water colour on a toned paper – 21,5 x 13,5 cm,
signed at the top right corner: Růža Zentner,
I skup. (group) 20 VI

page 56 (Inventory No 173 795)
UNKNOWN AUTHOR
Collage – 29,4 x 18,1 cm

page 57 (Inventory No 129 001)
MARIE FANTLOVÁ   born on 16. 10. 1930
deported to the Terezín ghetto on 2. 12. 1941,
deported from Terezín to Auschwitz on 23. 10. 1944.
Water colour – 29 x 21 cm, signed at the top right:
Marie Fantl 27

page 58 (Inventory No 133 055)
EVA HELLEROVÁ   born on 19.1. 1931
deported to the Terezín ghetto on 8. 9. 1942,
deported from Terezín to Auschwitz on 15. 12. 1943.
Collage on a form – 25 x 21 cm (after the painting „The nobleman and the lady drinking wine" by Vermeer van Delft), signed on the reverse side at the top left: Heller Eva Heim 11 (?)

page 59 (Inventory No 129 755)
RUTH GUTMANNOVÁ   born on 13. 4. 1930
deported to the Terezín ghetto on 17. 1. 1942,
deported from Terezín to Auschwitz on 6. 10. 1944.
Collage – 21 x 14,5 cm, signed: Gutmann Ruth – 220 Heim 28 13 Jahre

page 60 (Inventory No 130 934)
GUSTAV ZWEIG   born on 31. 7. 1930
deported to the Terezín ghetto on 8. 4. 1942,
deported from Terezín to Auschwitz on 4. 10. 1944.
Collage on a Czech military form – 29 x 24,5 cm, signed at the bottom margin: L 417 III Stunde VII A: 659 G.Zweig

page 62 (Inventory No 131 120)
MILAN BIENENFELD   born on 28. 3. 1930
deported to the Terezín ghetto on 24. 10. 1942,
deported from Terezín to Auschwitz on 18. 5. 1944.
Water colour on a toned paper – 34 x 21,5 cm, signed at the top right corner: Bienenfeld Milan, Heim II

page 63 (Inventory No 133 073)
UNKNOWN AUTHOR
Water colour on a sheet of paper, with a part of a technical drawing on the reverse side – 25 x 21 cm

page 64 (Inventory No 129 738)
RUTH SCHÄCHTEROVÁ   born on 24. 8. 1930
deported to the Terezín ghetto on 19. 3. 1942,
deported from Terezín to Auschwitz on 18. 5. 1944.
Collage on a coloured paper – 34 x 25 cm, signed at the top right: Ruth Schächterová

page 66 (Inventory No 129 450)
LEA POLLAKOVÁ   born on 21. 3. 1930
deported to the Terezín ghetto on 9. 12. 1942,
deported from Terezín to Auschwitz on 18. 5. 1944.
Collage – 34 x 26 cm, glued on 3 pieces of paper (toned paper and form), signed at the bottom left corner: Lea Pollak Heim 28

page 67 (Inventory No 131 296)
HANUŠ WEINBERG   born on 18. 8. 1931
deported to the Terezín ghetto on 5. 12. 1942,
deported from Terezín to Auschwitz on 15. 12. 1943.
Collage on a toned paper – 29,5 x 21 cm, signed on the reverse side: Hans Weinberg HEIM II, stunde 6

page 69 (Inventory No 131 651)
JOSEF NOVÁK   born on 25. 10. 1931
deported to the Terezín ghetto on 24. 4. 1942,
deported from Terezín to Auschwitz on 18. 5. 1944.
Water colour and pencil on a toned paper – 32 x 22 cm, signed at the top right: Novák Josef, HEIM X. STUNDE 20

page 70 (Inventory No 129 776)
DORIS WEISEROVÁ   born on 17. 5. 1932
deported to the Terezín ghetto on 30. 6. 1942,
deported from Terezín to Auschwitz on 4. 10. 1944.
Embroidery in wool on a form – 17,5 x 14,5 cm, signed at the top right corner: Doris Weiser

page 72 (Inventory No 129 528)
JIŘÍ RIES   born on 4. 9. 1933
deported to the Terezín ghetto on 30. 6. 1942,
deported from Terezín to Auschwitz on 4. 10. 1944.
Water colour on a toned paper – 29 x 22,5 cm, signed at the top right: Ries Jirka Gruppe 5.11.26.VI.

page 74 (Inventory No 130 584)
GABI FREIOVÁ   born on 1. 1. 1933
deported to the Terezín ghetto on 9. 12. 1942,
deported from Terezín to Auschwitz on 18. 5. 1944.
Pastel – 25 x 20 cm, signed at the top right: Gabi Freiová Heim 13.I.1944

page 75 (Inventory No 130 800)
ANITA SPITZOVÁ   born on 6. 1. 1933
deported to the Terezín ghetto on 10. 12. 1941,
deported from Terezín to Auschwitz on 4. 10. 1944.
Pastel – 32 x 22 cm, signed at the top left: II skup. (group) 12.III. and at the top right: Anita Spitzová II 12.IV.

page 76 (Inventory No 125 523)
HANUŠ FISCHL   born on 26. 9. 1933
deported to the Terezín ghetto on 10. 12. 1941,
deported from Terezín to Auschwitz on 6. 10. 1944.
Pastel – 29,5 x 20 cm, signed at the bottom left: 24/IV Fischl 44, at the bottom right: II Gruppe Hons, with a drawing in pencil and pastel at the reverse side, at the top right: FISCHL HONS, Gruppe II 24/IV 44

EDITOR'S COMMENTS TO THE POEMS

page 7
PAVEL FRIEDMANN   born on 7. 1. 1921
deported to the Terezín ghetto on 28. 4. 1942,
deported from Terezín to Auschwitz on 29. 9. 1944.

The verse „The Butterfly" was typewritten together with other verses on a sheet of paper size
A3. It is not possible to specify, whether it is
a copy from Terezín or a later one. It is dated at
the top left: 4.6. 1942.

page 13
„TEDDY"   author unknown

The verse „At Terezín" exists only in a typewritten version. It is not possible to specify, whether
it is a copy from Terezín. There is a note at the
bottom left: 1943, bottom right: Teddy.
Underneath in pencil handwriting: L 410.

page 14
MIROSLAV KOŠEK   born on 30. 3. 1932
deported to the Terezín ghetto on 26. 2. 1942,
deported from Terezín to Auschwitz on 19. 10. 1944.

The verse „It all depends on how you look at it"
exists in original handwriting. It was written in
child's handwriting in ink on a blank side of
a form, torn from a writing pad. At the top left in
the same handwriting: Mir. Košek. On the other
side, in the lines of the form, are filled some
columns in child's handwriting: Marmelade,
Zukr etc.

page 16
KOLÉBA is an abbreviation of three child authors:
MIROSLAV KOŠEK   see page 14
HANUŠ LÖWY   born on 29. 6. 1931
deported to the Terezín ghetto on 30. 9. 1942,
deported from Terezín to Auschwitz on 4. 10. 1944.
BACHNER   no further data are known,
the author has most probably survived.

The verse „Man proposes, God disposes" exists
only in a typewritten version.
At the top left in pencil handwriting: 25/II, top
right in adult's handwriting: Mir.Košek. Below
the text of the verse: Koléba: Košek, Löwy,
Bachner, 5.

page 21
The verse „Pain strikes sparks on me, the pain of
Terezín" by an unknown author, is written together with other four verses on one list of yellowed paper, probably torn from a writing pad. It

is in original handwriting but it looks like an
adult's handwriting. There are no notes on the
page.

page 22, 23
HANUŠ HACHENBURG   born on 12. 7. 1929
deported to the Terezín ghetto on 24. 10. 1942,
deported from Terezín to Auschwitz on 18. 12. 1943.
After half year's stay at the camp B IIb in Birkenau, in
the so-called family camp, he died between
10. – 12. 7. 1944 in a gas chamber.

The original of the verse „Terezín" exists in the
children's Terezín journal „Vedem", edited by
the children at home I. at L 417. The journal
„Vedem" is in the collection of the Terezín
Memorial.

page 24
KOLÉBA   see page 16

The verse „Yes, that's the way things are" exists
in the original, in the same child's handwriting
as the verse „It depends" by Miroslav Košek. It is
written on a blank side of a yellowed page of a
form in faded ink. Under the text is in the same
handwriting: Koléba: Košek, Löwy, Bachner.

page 29
KOLÉBA   see page 16

The verse „The Little mouse" exists in original
child's handwriting in ink on a blank side of
a form. At the top right corner in the same handwriting: Koléba: Košek, Löwy, Bachner.

page 30
The verse „Homesick" by an unknown author,
exists in original, written in child's handwriting
in pencil, on both sides of a yellowed lined paper, probably torn from an exercise book. At the
top right in the same handwriting: 9.III. 1943.

page 35
The verse „Night in the ghetto" by an unknown
author, is written together with two other verses
in an original child's handwriting in ink, on
a sheet of paper size A4. Under the verse in the
same handwriting: 1943. At the bottom right:
L 410.

page 36
HANUŠ HACHENBURG   see page 22, 23

The original of the verse „Questions, and an an-
swer" is in the journal „Vedem" – see page 22, 23.

page 37
EVA PICKOVÁ   born on 15. 5. 1929
deported to the Terezín ghetto on 16. 4. 1942, from
Terezín to Auschwitz on 18. 12. 1943.

The verse „Fear" exists in a typewritten form
and it is not possible to state, if it was typed in
Terezín or at a later time. Under the text of the
verse is written: 12 letá Eva Picková z Nymburka
(Eva Picková from Nymburk, 12 years old).

page 43
ALENA SYNKOVÁ   born on 24. 9. 1926
deported to the Terezín ghetto on 22. 12. 1942,
she has survived.

The verse „To Olga" exists in original. It is written in the author's handwriting, in pencil (very
faded today), on a narrow sheet of paper.
There is another verse written on the back of
this sheet. Under the verse in a different handwriting: L 410.

page 45
ZDENĚK OHRENSTEIN   born on 10. 1. 1929
deported to the Terezín ghetto on 24. 10. 1942,
deported from Terezín to Auschwitz and other concentration camps – he has survived.
After the war he was the famous Prague actor Zdeněk
Ornest. He died in Prague on 4. 11. 1990.

The verse „Forgotten" exists in the original
handwriting. It is written in faded ink on a small
sheet of paper, without any notes. The verse was
originally considered to be written by an unknown author.

page 47
FRANTIŠEK BASS   born on 4. 9. 1930
deported to the Terezín ghetto on 2. 12. 1941,
deported from Terezín to Auschwitz on 28. 10. 1944.

The verse „The Garden" was written on one
sheet of paper together with other verses
(see page 54, 55). It is in adult's handwriting in
ink on yellowed paper. It is not possible to state
the time of its origin. The author's name appears
between the verses.

page 54, 55
FRANTIŠEK BASS and the data about the verses – see
page 47.

page 61
HANUŠ HACHENBURG   see page 22, 23
The original of the verse „Reflections" is written
in the journal „Vedem" – see page 22, 23.

page 65
ALENA SYNKOVÁ   see page 43
The verse „I'd like to go away alone" is written
in original handwriting in pencil on a narrow
sheet of paper, together with two other verses.

The paper is yellowed, the writing very faded.
On the bottom right there is written in the same
handwriting in ink: Alena Synková.

page 68
The verse by an unknown author „Birdsong" is
written together with other verses – see page 35
– under the verse is noted later: 1941.

page 71
ZDENĚK OHRENSTEIN   see page 45.
The original of the verse „While..." is written
together with other verses by the same author
on one small sheet of paper in faded ink. There
are no comments on the text and it has been
considered to be written by an unknown author
until recent time.

page 73
IVO LEO KATZ   born on 11. 4. 1932
deported to the Terezín ghetto on 13. 7. 1943,
deported from Terezín to Auschwitz on 18. 12. 1943.

The verse „Some day" is written in original
child's handwriting in ink on both sides of one
sheet of paper. The paper has been slightly crum-
pled and torn. Under the text of the verse is
a note, dated probably after the liberation:
Terezín 1943 – Ivo Katz, born 1932.

page 77
ZDENĚK OHRENSTEIN – the data concerning the
verse „The poor thing " – see page 45 and 71.

With the exception of the verses by Hanuš Hachenburg
all the published verses are kept at the Jewish Museum
in Prague in the collection „Terezín", the verse by
Pavel Friedmann under the inventory No 326, the others under the inventory No 325.

CONTENTS

Translated into English by Joy Kadečková, Jeanne Němcová and Edith Pargeretová – further J. K., J. N., E. P.

I HAVE NOT SEEN A BUTTERFLY
AROUND HERE

CHILDREN'S DRAWINGS AND POEMS
FROM TEREZÍN

Based on the book "Children's Drawings and Poems – Terezín 1942 – 1944",
edited by Hana Volavková of the State Jewish Museum in Prague in 1959, prepared for publication
by Anita Franková and Hana Povolná.

The foreword by Jiří Weil reprinted from the 1959 edition.
The postscript by Anita Franková.

The drawings and poems selected and arranged by Anita Franková, Ludmila Kybalová and Hana Povolná.
Editor's comments by Anita Franková and Hana Povolná.

Translation: Joy Kadečková, Jeanne Němcová and Edith Pargeretová
Photographs: Jewish Museum Prague   Layout: Pavel Šváb and Václav Toušek
Publisher: The Jewish Museum Prague at the REAG Prague, 1993
Printed by Tiskárna Flora, s.r.o.
First edition, reprint 1994
© The Jewish Museum Prague 1993